Why Manners Matter

Going Shopping

Jillian Powell

W

FRANKLIN WATTS

LONDON • SYDNEY

First published in 2005 by
Franklin Watts
96 Leonard Street
London
EC2A 4XD

Franklin Watts Australia
45-51 Huntley Street
Alexandria, NSW 2015

© Franklin Watts 2005

Editor: Rachel Tonkin
Series design: Mo Choy
Art director: Jonathan Hair
Photography: Chris Fairclough
Photograph on page 20 kindly supplied by Waitrose Ltd
PSHE Consultant: Wendy Anthony

A CIP catalogue record for this book is
available from the British Library

ISBN: 0 7496 6049 X

Printed in Hong Kong

KNOWSLEY LIBRARY SERVICE

Knowsl@y Council

Please return this book on or before the date shown below

PROJECT LOAN

Contents

At the shops

Going shopping is fun.
Most people you meet
are polite and kind.

It's important to be polite
and kind to others, too.
This makes shopping safer
and nicer for everyone.

? How often do
you go shopping?

Waiting for a bus

E2

LONDON
UNITED
BUS STOP
Eden Street

towards Kingston Hospital
or New Malden

57	85	131
213	514	K2
K3	K5	K9
K10	N77	N213

You often have to wait in a queue when you catch a bus. It's not fair to push in front of other people.

? What happens if everyone tries to get on the bus at the same time?

Take care

You should never run around near busy roads or try to cross them without an adult.

Shops are busy places, too.
If you run around or play games,
you may hurt yourself or others.

Be careful

Being helpful

There are lots of ways to help people when you are shopping.

You can hold the door open for someone with a pram.

Can I help?

You can help your family, too, by carrying some of their shopping bags.

Magic words

When you ask for something in a shop, always remember to ask politely and say please.

If someone buys you a present, you should say thank you and show them how pleased you are.

? How do you feel if someone forgets to say please and thank you?

Be patient

Sometimes you have to wait
to be served.

You need to be quiet and patient while you wait your turn. This helps the shop assistant.

Wait your turn

? What would happen if everyone tried to push in front at the checkout?

Tidying up

A shopping centre is for everyone to share. You don't want to spoil it by dropping litter. Put your rubbish in the bin.

use the bin!

? What would happen if no-one bothered to use the litter bins?

17

Being polite

When you're out shopping, say excuse me when you need to get past.

Shopping can be tiring. But there may be someone who needs to sit down more than you do.

Would you like a seat?

A smile

Shop workers have long and busy days. You can help to make their day better by saying hello and goodbye.

Bye, bye

? Why do you think people like it when you smile?

If you smile, you may get a
smile back, which will make
your day better, too.

Think about . . .

When you are crossing the road, there are lots of things you should think about . . .

? What should you do before you cross the road?

? Why should you hold on to your parent's hand when you cross the road?

? What might happen if you ran around near a busy road?

Think about why manners are important when you are in a busy supermarket . . .

? How do you ask a shop assistant where something is in the supermarket?

? What happens if you run around in a busy shop?

? What do you say if you need to get past someone in a supermarket?

? What do you say to the checkout person when you leave the shop?

Index